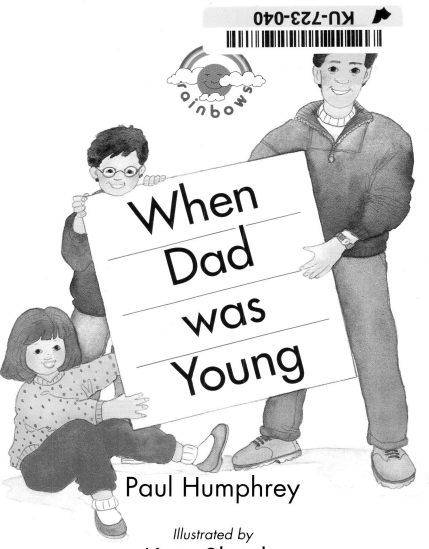

When Dad was Young

Paul Humphrey

Illustrated by
Katy Sleight

I did lots of things.
Now, let me think.

5

6

Yes, but the pictures were
only black and white.

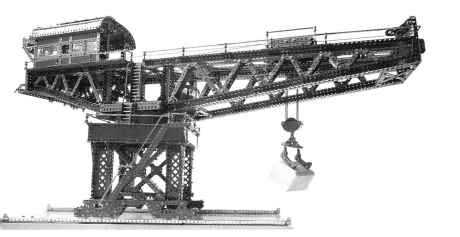

My toys looked like this. My
favourite was Meccano.

Did you ride a bike when you were young, Dad?

Yes. My bike looked like this.
It was called a chopper.

What were cars like when you were young, Dad?

12

When I was young, cars looked like this. I had to help clean my dad's car.

When I was 5, I watched the TV to see the first man walk on the Moon.

I'd like to be an astronaut.

15

When I was a teenager we wore clothes like these.

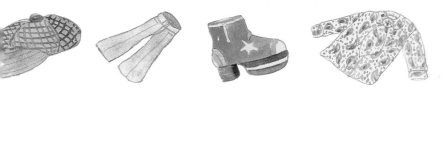

17

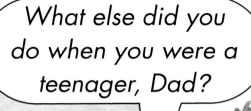

18

I played my records.

19

Sometimes I went to a disco.

20

21

I listened to pop music
on my transistor radio.

That's a funny radio.

23

When I was 14, I saw the first Concorde fly past.

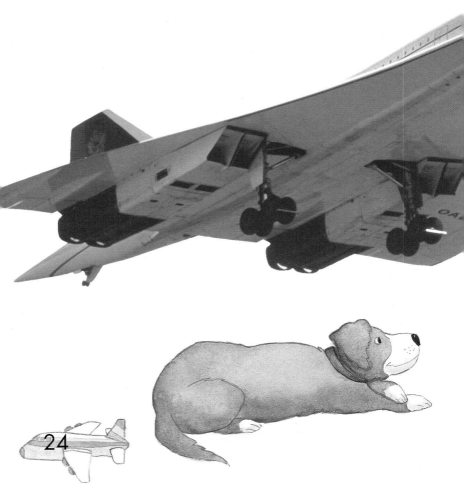

I would like to
fly in Concorde.

When I was 16, I had a
motorbike.

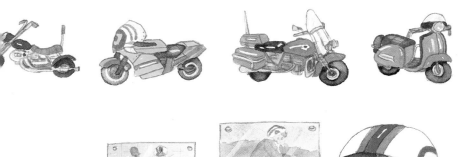

27

When you are a dad you can tell your children about all the things you did when you were young.

Yes, I'll have lots to tell them.

29

Which of the things on this page belong to Dad's time and which belong to today?